STEP-BY-STEP
Math Readiness

LINWORTH
LEARNING

From the Minds of Teachers

Linworth Publishing, Inc.
Worthington, Ohio

Cataloging-in-Publication Data

Editor: Claire Morris

Design and Production: Good Neighbor Press, Inc.

Published by Linworth Publishing, Inc.
480 East Wilson Bridge Road, Suite L
Worthington, Ohio 43085

ISBN: 1-58683-143-7

5 4 3 2 1

Table of Contents

 # Introduction

The goal of this book is mastery of the skills necessary for computational fluency. The mastery of these skills is achieved through meaningful, step-by-step practice exercises emphasizing number recognition, counting, ordering, comparing, shape recognition, and pattern prediction. Central to the structure of the book is the knowledge that a foundation of certain skills is necessary for mathematical understanding. Children will move sequentially through the step-by-step exercises in this book, building on their ability to solve everyday mathematical operations. The material in *Step-by-Step Math Readiness* correlates with the national curriculum standards for numbers and operations for the Pre-K–2 student set by the National Council of Teachers of Math. An answer key is provided at the back of the book.

 # Number 1

Directions: Practice writing the number and number word.

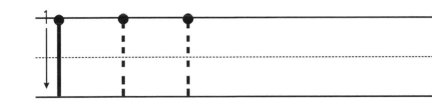

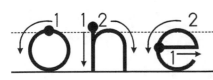 

Name_____   Date_____

Number 2

Directions: Practice writing the number and number word.

2

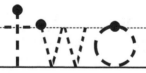

Number 3

Directions: Practice writing the number and number word.

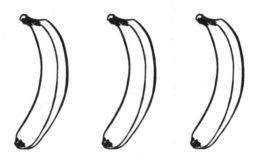

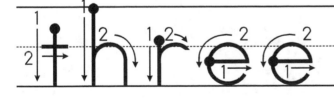

Number 4

Directions: Practice writing the number and number word.

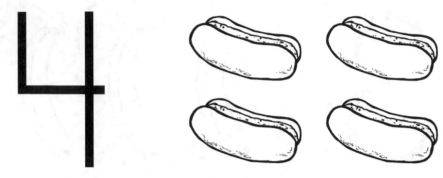

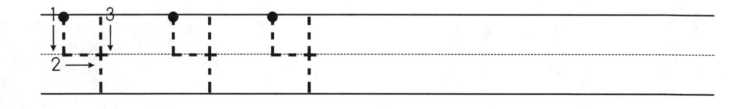

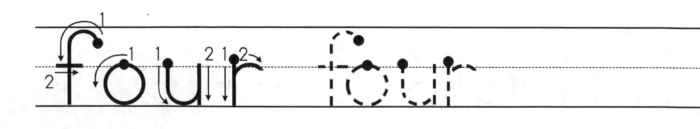

Name_____ Date_____

 # Number 5

Directions: Practice writing the number and number word.

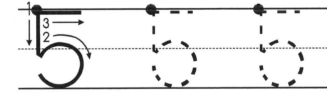

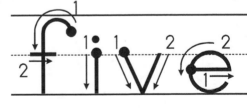 

Number 6

Directions: Practice writing the number and number word.

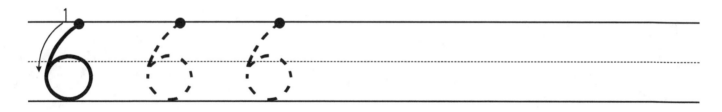

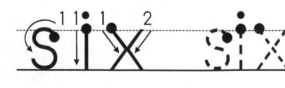

 Number 7

Directions: Practice writing the number and number word.

7

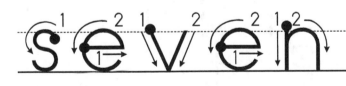

Name_____ Date_____

Number 8

Directions: Practice writing the number and number word.

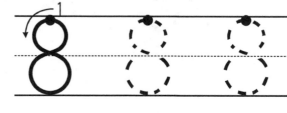

 Number 9

Directions: Practice writing the number and number word.

q

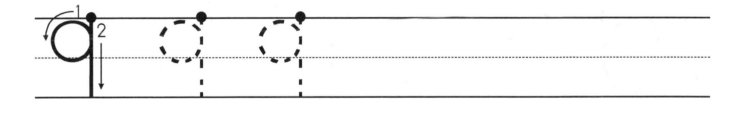

 # Number 10

Directions: Practice writing the number and number word.

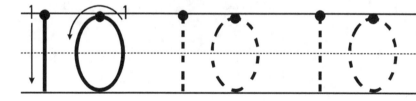

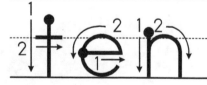 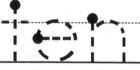

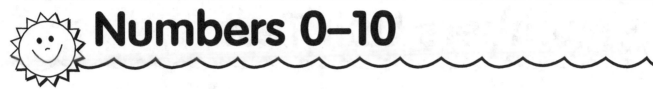

Numbers 0–10

Directions: Start on the dot to trace each number.

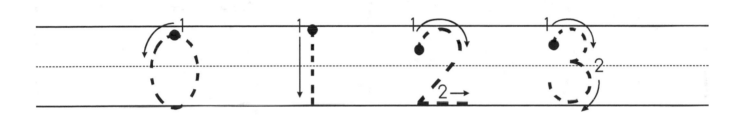

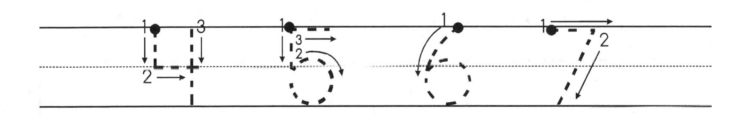

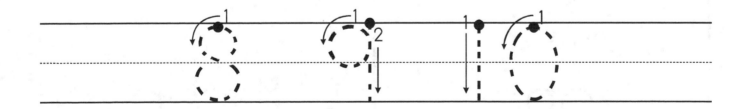

 Numbers Unit Test

Directions: Fill in the circle next to the matching number.

two

○ 3   ○ 2   ○ 1

four

○ 4   ○ 2   ○ 3

one

○ 2   ○ 3   ○ 1

three

○ 2   ○ 1   ○ 3

Name_____ Date_____

 # Numbers Unit Test

Directions: Fill in the circle next to the matching number.

five

○ 5   ○ 3   ○ 4

nine

○ 6   ○ 9   ○ 7

zero

○ 2   ○ 0   ○ 1

seven

○ 9   ○ 8   ○ 7

Numbers Unit Test

Directions: Fill in the circle next to the matching number.

six

○ 4   ○ 8   ○ 6

eight

○ 9   ○ 8   ○ 6

four

○ 4   ○ 6   ○ 2

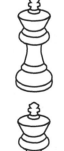 

ten

○ 10   ○ 9   ○ 7

Counting

Directions: Color or circle the correct number of pictures in each row.

0	🐦 🐦 🐦 🐦 🐦
1	🐁 🐁 🐁 🐁 🐁
2	🐟 🐟 🐟 🐟 🐟
3	🦊 🦊 🦊 🦊 🦊
4	🦉 🦉 🦉 🦉 🦉
5	🐞 🐞 🐞 🐞 🐞

Counting

Directions: Color or circle the correct number of pictures in each row.

2	(computers)
5	(alarm clocks)
0	(televisions)
4	(telephones)
1	(cell phones)
3	(tape players)

Counting

Directions: Color or circle the correct number of pictures in each row.

6	
7	
8	
9	
10	

Counting

Directions: Color or circle the correct number of pictures in each row.

7	
2	
5	
8	
6	
10	
3	

Name_____ Date_____

 # Counting

Directions: Count the pictures in each box, and write the number on the line.

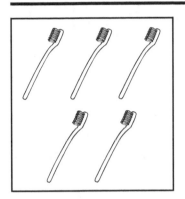  _____

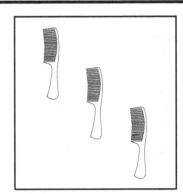 _____

 _____

_____

 _____

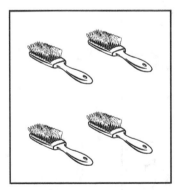 _____

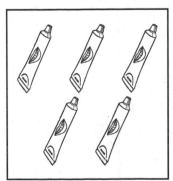 _____

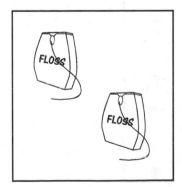 _____

☀ Counting

Directions: Count the pictures in each box, and write the number on the line.

   7

   _____

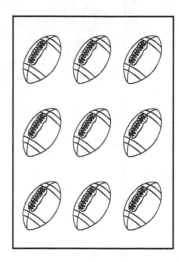   _____

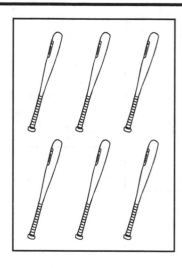   _____

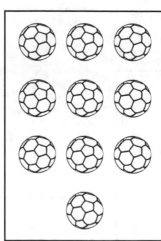   _____

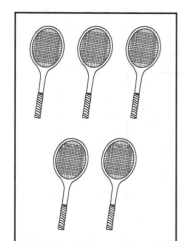   _____

☀ Counting

Directions: Draw a line from each number to the matching number of pictures.

4

1

5

2

3

 # Counting

Directions: Draw a line from each number to the matching number of pictures.

7

9

6

10

8

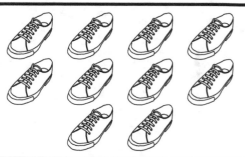

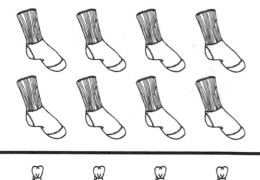

 # Counting

Directions: Count the pictures in the box, and write the number you find for each picture.

 _____

 _____

 _____

 _____

 _____

 _____

 _____

Counting

Directions: Count the pictures in the box, and write the number you find for each picture.

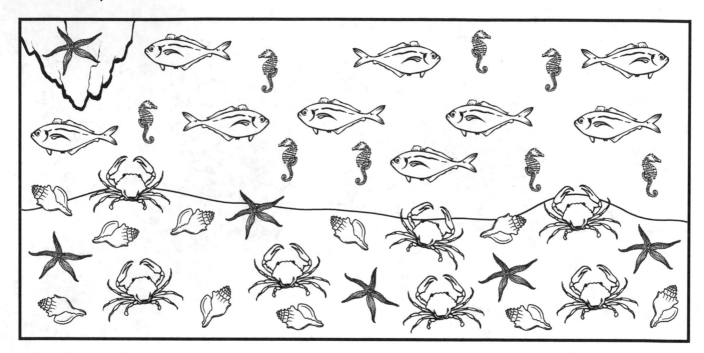

_____

_____

_____

_____

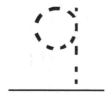 
_____

Counting Unit Test

Directions: Count the pictures, and fill in the circle next to the correct number.

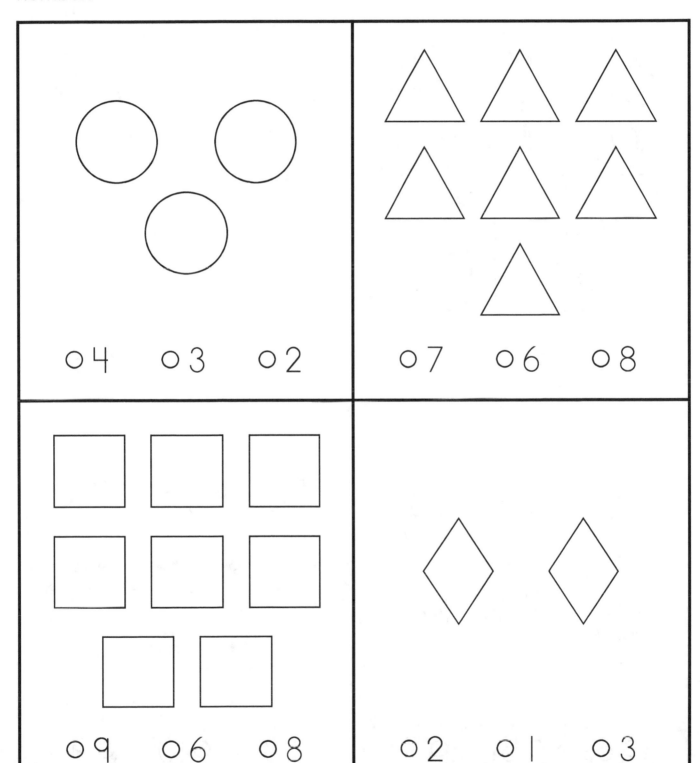

○ 4   ○ 3   ○ 2

○ 7   ○ 6   ○ 8

○ 9   ○ 6   ○ 8

○ 2   ○ 1   ○ 3

☀ Counting Unit Test

Directions: Count the pictures, and fill in the circle next to the correct number.

○ 3   ○ 2   ○ 5

○ 6   ○ 9   ○ 8

○ 6   ○ 5   ○ 7

○ 8   ○ 10   ○ 9

Counting Unit Test

Directions: Fill in the circle next to the number of times the picture appears in the box.

o 2   o 4   o 3   o 2   o 1   o 3

o 2   o 4   o 5   o 5   o 4   o 3

Ordering

Directions: Fill in the missing numbers.

0 1 2 _3_ 4 5 6 7 8 9 10

0 1 _ 3 4 5 _ 7 8 9 10

0 1 2 3 4 5 6 _ 8 9 _

0 _ 2 3 4 _ 6 7 _ 9 10

__ 1 2 3 _ 5 6 7 8 _ 10

Ordering

Directions: Connect the dots in order from 1 to 10.

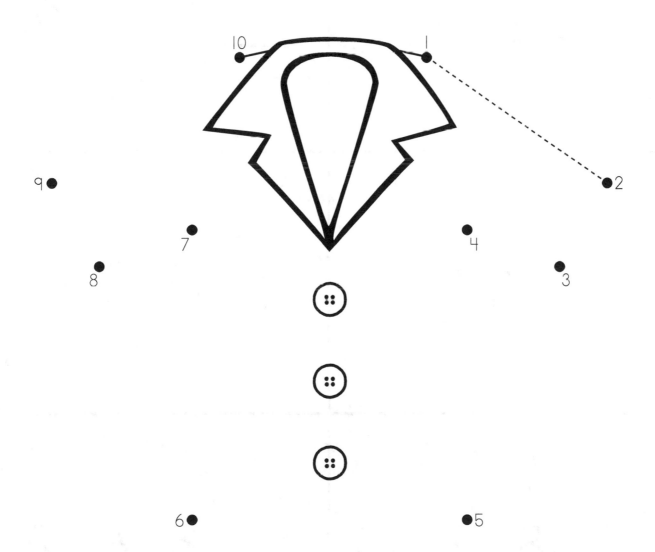

Ordering

Directions: Fill in the missing numbers.

1, 2, 3, 4	__, 7, 8, 9
__, 3, 4, 5	__, 4, 5, 6
__, 8, 9, 10	__, 5, 6, 7

Ordering

Directions: Fill in the missing numbers.

2, 3, 4, 5	3, 4, 5, __
0, 1, 2, __	7, 8, 9, __
4, 5, 6, __	6, 7, 8, __

 Ordering

Directions: Look at each number, and circle the picture that is in that position.

1st	
2nd	
3rd	
4th	
5th	
6th	

 Ordering

Directions: Draw the picture that is in each listed position.

? $! + =

3rd __________   **5**th _____

1st _____   **2**nd _____

4th _____

Name_____ Date_____

☀ Comparing

Directions: Circle the greater number.

Directions: Circle the smaller number.

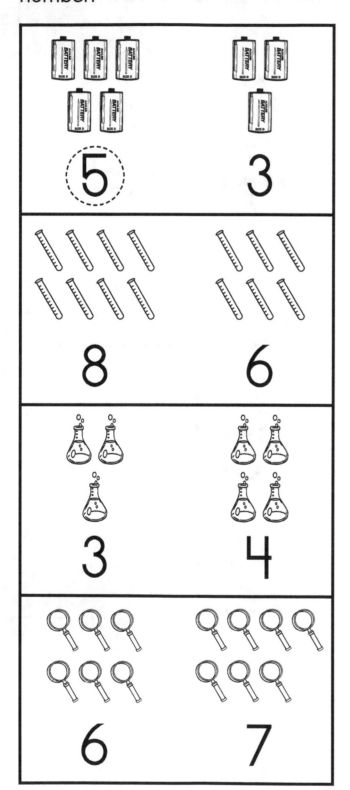

(5)	3
8	6
3	4
6	7

6	(5)
2	4
9	7
3	8

 Comparing

Directions: Circle the group that has more.

Comparing

Directions: Circle the group that has less.

Ordering and Comparing Unit Test

Directions: Fill in the circle next to the missing number.

0, 1, 2, __, 4	1, __, 3, 4, 5
○3　　○5　　○4	○4　　○2　　○0
__, 2, 3, 4, 5	3, 4, 5, 6, __
○1　　○2　　○0	○9　　○8　　○7

Name_____ Date_____

Ordering and Comparing Unit Test

Directions: Fill in the circle next to the missing number.

7, 8, __, 10	__, 7, 8, 9
○ 5 ○ 7 ○ 9	○ 7 ○ 6 ○ 4
7, 8, 9, __	5, 6, 7, __
○ 10 ○ 9 ○ 6	○ 6 ○ 8 ○ 7

Name_____   Date_____

 # Ordering and Comparing Unit Test

Directions: Fill in the circle next to the group that has the most pictures.

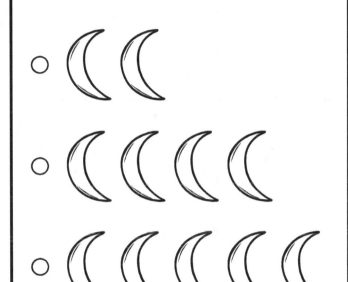

Shapes

Directions: Color the matching shape in each row.

Shapes

Directions: Color the circles.

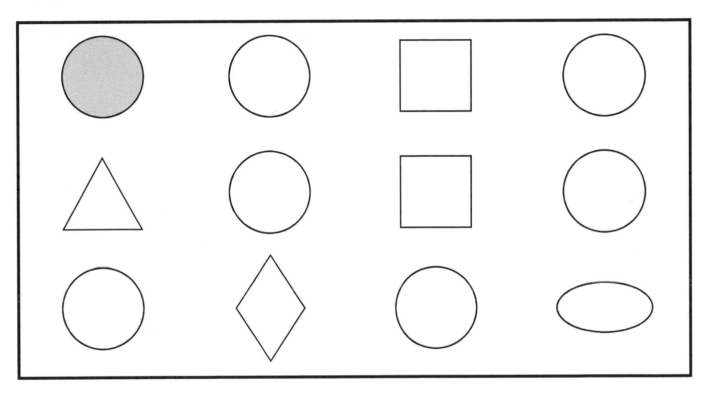

Directions: Color the ovals.

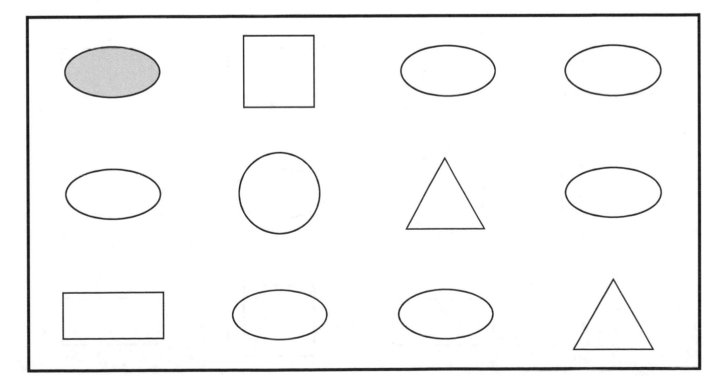

Shapes

Directions: Color the squares.

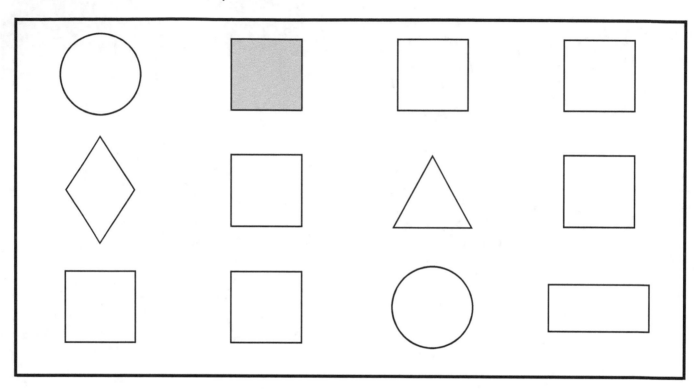

Directions: Color the rectangles.

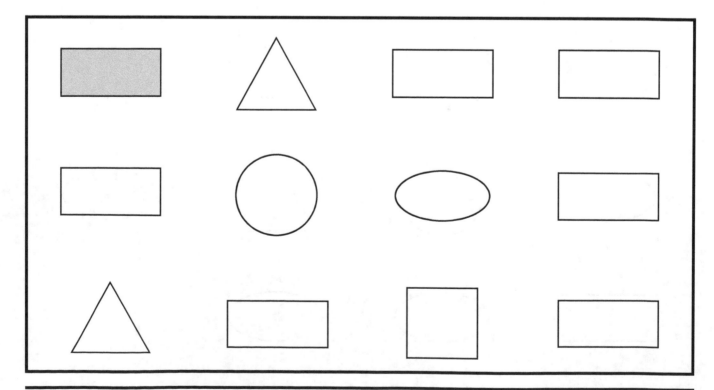

Shapes

Directions: Color the triangles.

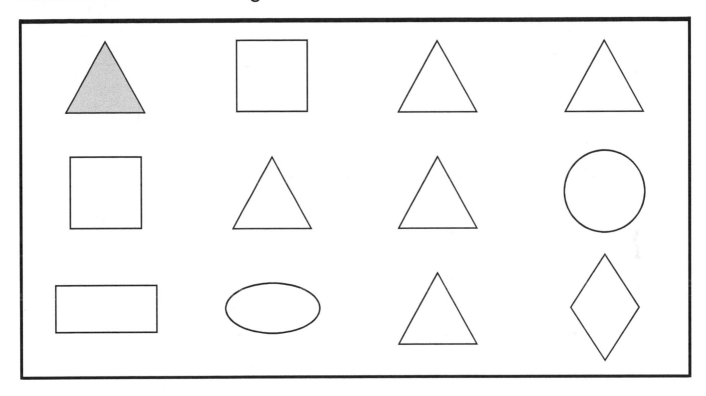

Directions: Color the diamonds.

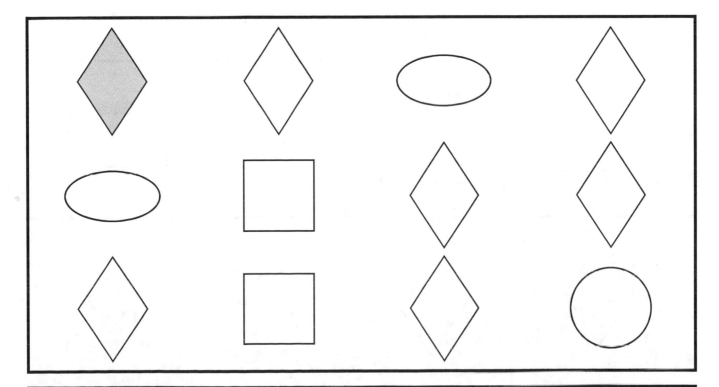

Shapes

Directions: Cross out the shape that does not match in each row.

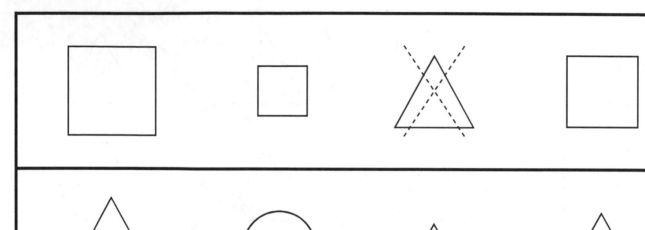

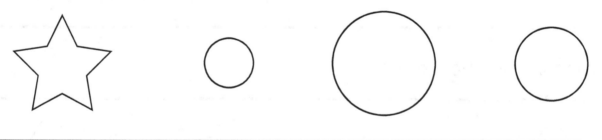

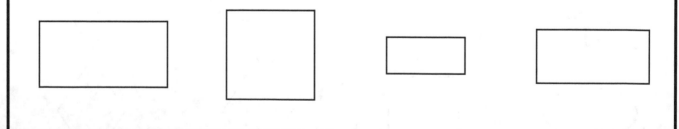

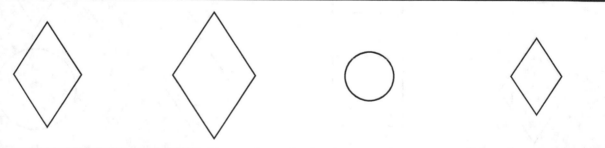

Shapes

Directions: Circle the pictures that are the same shape in each row.

 Shapes

Directions: Color the matching shape in each row.

Copyright © 2003 Linworth Publishing, Inc.

Shapes

Directions: Circle the pictures that are the same shape in each row.

Shapes

Directions: Color the shapes the correct colors.

Color the ☐ blue.

Color the ◯ yellow.

Color the △ green.

Color the ▭ red.

Name_____ Date_____

Shapes and Patterns Unit Test

Directions: Fill in the circle next to the matching shape.

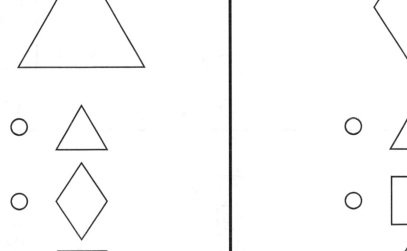

Shapes and Patterns Unit Test

Directions: Fill in the circle under the shape that does not match.

Name_____ Date_____

 # Shapes and Patterns Unit Test

Directions: Fill in the circle next to the shape that would come next in the pattern.

 Final Assessment

Directions: Fill in the circle next to the matching number.

two

○ 3   ○ 2   ○ 1

four

○ 4   ○ 5   ○ 3

six

○ 5   ○ 3   ○ 6

eight

○ 6   ○ 8   ○ 9

Name_____ Date_____

 # Final Assessment

Directions: Count the pictures, and fill in the circle next to the correct number.

○ 6　　○ 3　　○ 5

○ 7　　○ 5　　○ 6

○ 4　　○ 3　　○ 1

○ 10　　○ 7　　○ 8

Name_____ Date_____

Final Assessment

Directions: Fill in the circle next to the correct answer.

Which number is missing?

7, __, 9, 10

○ 6   ○ 8   ○ 9

Which number is missing?

2, 3, 4, __

○ 5   ○ 6   ○ 1

Which has the most?

○

Which has the least?

Answer Key pages 1–9

Number 1

Name_____ Date_____

Directions: Practice writing the number and number word.

1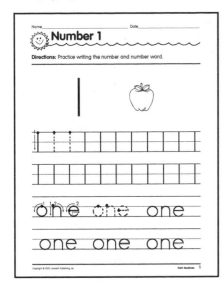

one one one
one one one

Number 2

Name_____ Date_____

Directions: Practice writing the number and number word.

2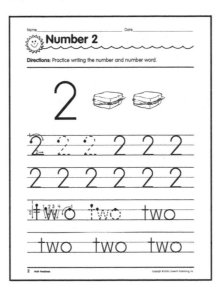

2 2 2 2 2 2
2 2 2 2 2 2
two two two
two two two

Number 3

Name_____ Date_____

Directions: Practice writing the number and number word.

3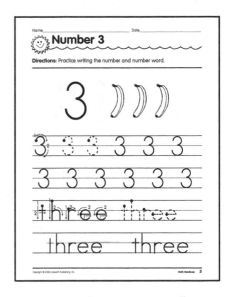

3 3 3 3 3 3
3 3 3 3 3 3
three three
three three

Number 4

Name_____ Date_____

Directions: Practice writing the number and number word.

4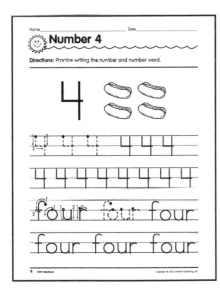

4 4 4 4
4 4 4 4 4 4
four four four
four four four

Number 5

Name_____ Date_____

Directions: Practice writing the number and number word.

5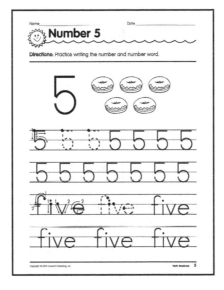

5 5 5 5 5 5
5 5 5 5 5 5
five five five
five five five

Number 6

Name_____ Date_____

Directions: Practice writing the number and number word.

6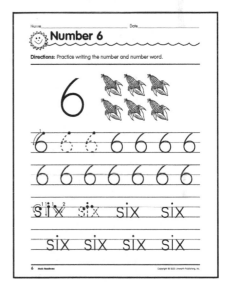

6 6 6 6 6 6
6 6 6 6 6 6
six six six six
six six six six

Number 7

Name_____ Date_____

Directions: Practice writing the number and number word.

7

7 7 7 7 7 7
7 7 7 7 7 7
seven seven
seven seven

Number 8

Name_____ Date_____

Directions: Practice writing the number and number word.

8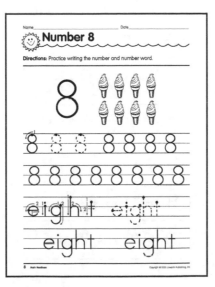

8 8 8 8 8 8
8 8 8 8 8 8
eight eight
eight eight

Number 9

Name_____ Date_____

Directions: Practice writing the number and number word.

9

9 9 9 9 9 9
9 9 9 9 9 9
nine nine nine
nine nine nine

Answer Key pages 10–18

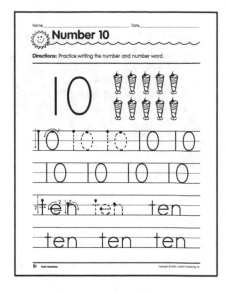

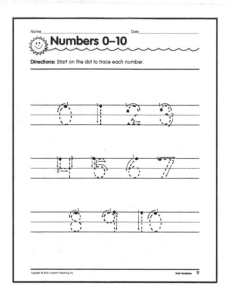

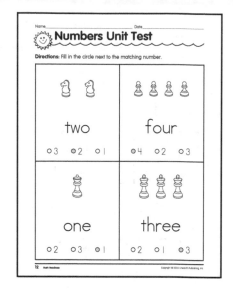

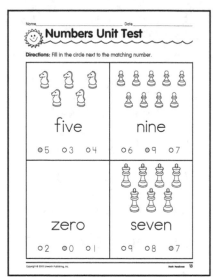

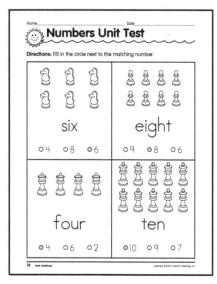

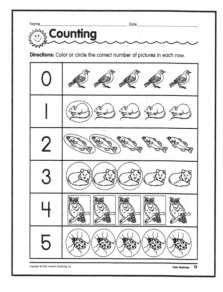

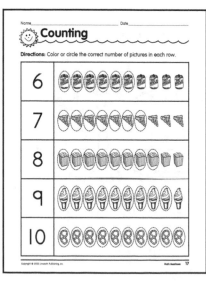

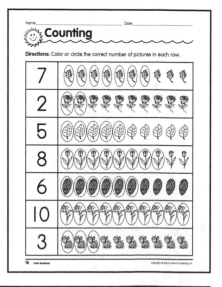

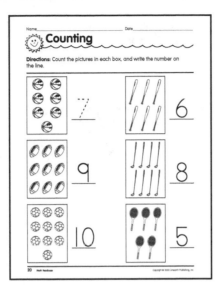

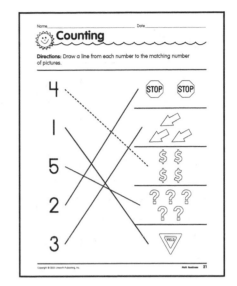

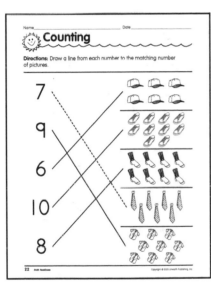

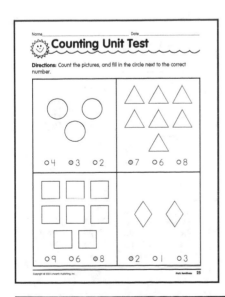

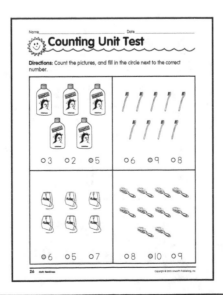

Answer Key pages 28–36

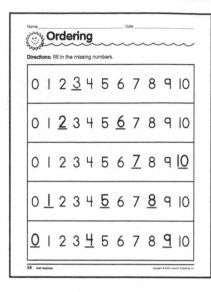

Ordering

Directions: Fill in the missing numbers.

0 1 2 **3** 4 5 6 7 8 9 10
0 1 **2** 3 4 5 **6** 7 8 9 10
0 1 2 3 4 5 6 **7** 8 9 **10**
0 **1** 2 3 4 **5** 6 7 **8** 9 10
0 1 2 3 **4** 5 6 7 8 **9** 10

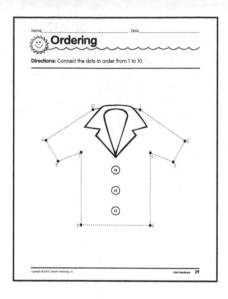

Ordering

Directions: Connect the dots in order from 1 to 10.

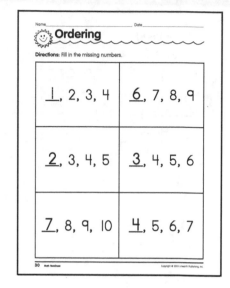

Ordering

Directions: Fill in the missing numbers.

1, 2, 3, 4	**6**, 7, 8, 9
2, 3, 4, 5	**3**, 4, 5, 6
7, 8, 9, 10	**4**, 5, 6, 7

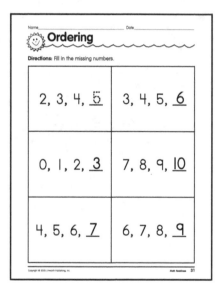

Ordering

Directions: Fill in the missing numbers.

2, 3, 4, **5**	3, 4, 5, **6**
0, 1, 2, **3**	7, 8, 9, **10**
4, 5, 6, **7**	6, 7, 8, **9**

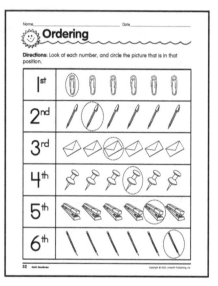

Ordering

Directions: Look at each number, and circle the picture that is in that position.

1st	
2nd	
3rd	
4th	
5th	
6th	

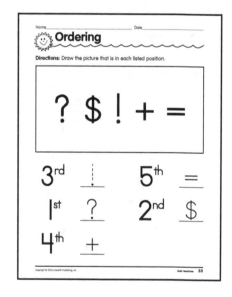

Ordering

Directions: Draw the picture that is in each listed position.

? $! + =

3rd :
5th =
1st ?
2nd $
4th +

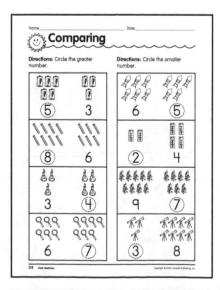

Comparing

Directions: Circle the greater number.

Directions: Circle the smaller number.

5 3   6 **5**
8 6   **2** 4
3 **4**   9 **7**
6 **7**   **3** 8

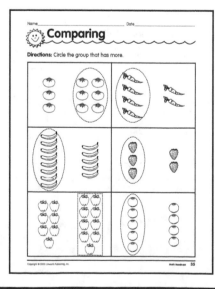

Comparing

Directions: Circle the group that has more.

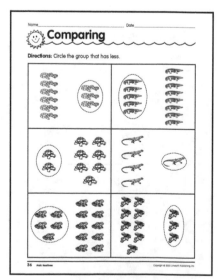

Comparing

Directions: Circle the group that has less.

Answer Key   pages 37–45

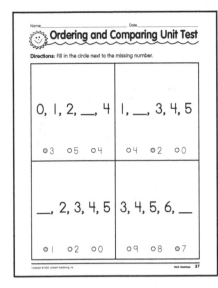

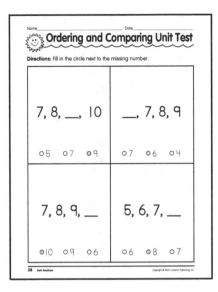

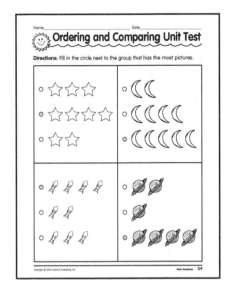

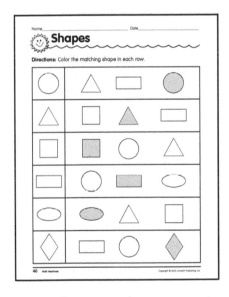

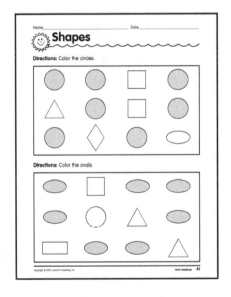

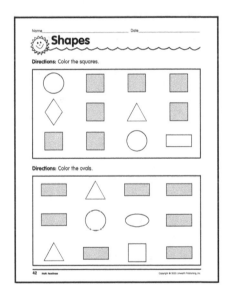

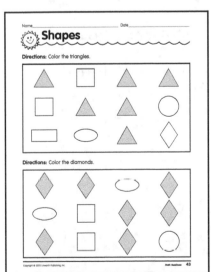

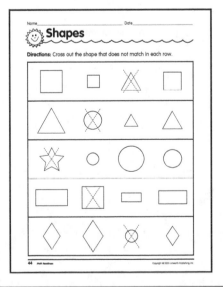

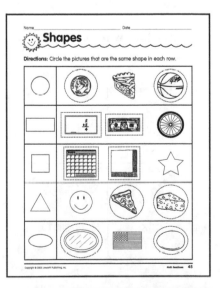

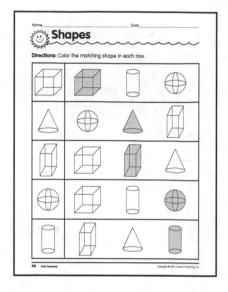
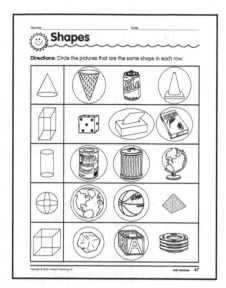
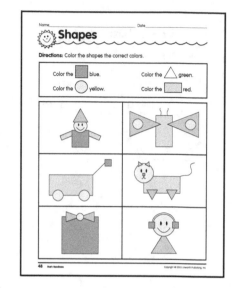
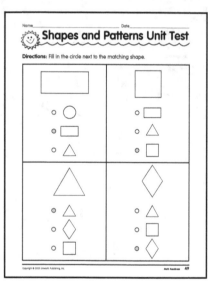
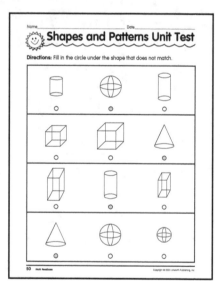
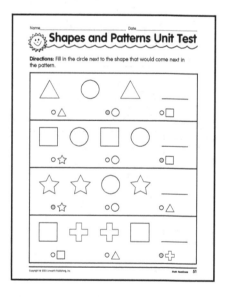
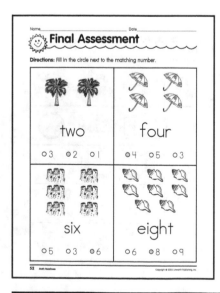
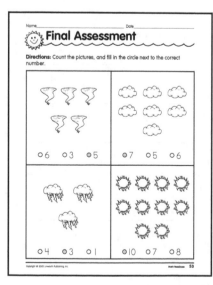
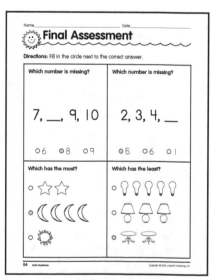